KIDS ON EARTH

Wildlife Adventures – Explore The World
Mouse Lemur - Madagascar

Sensei Paul David

COPYRIGHT PAGE

Kids On Earth: Wildlife Adventures - Explore The World

Blue Morpho Butterfly - Costa Rica Mouse Lemur - Madagascar

by Sensei Paul David,

Copyright © 2023.

All rights reserved.

978-1-77848-175-8 KoE_WildLife_Amazon_PaperbackBook_madagascar_mouse lemur

978-1-77848-174-1 KoE_WildLife_Amazon_eBook_madagascar_mouse lemur

978-1-77848-418-6 KoE_Wildlife_Ingram_Paperbackbook_MouseLemur

This book is not authorized for free distribution copying.

www.senseipublishing.com

@senseipublishing
#senseipublishing

Synopsis

This book introduces readers to the mouse lemur, the smallest primate in the world. It presents 30 fun facts about this fascinating animal and its unique habitat, including its small size, nocturnal habits, omnivorous diet, and ability to survive in the wild. It also discusses the importance of mouse lemurs to the health of the ecosystems in which they live. The book concludes by emphasizing the importance of this species to Madagascar's biodiversity.

Get Our FREE Books Now!

kidsonearth.life

kidsonearth.world

Click Below for Another Book In Each Series

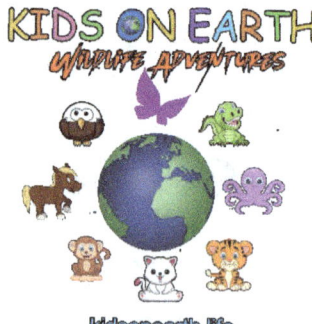

senseipublishing.com/KoE_SERIES

senseipublishing.com/KoE_Wildlife_SERIES

KoE En Español

senseipublishing.com/KoE_SERIES_SPANISH

www.senseipublishing.com

Join Our Publishing Journey!

If you would like to receive FUTURE FREE BOOKS and get to know us better, please click www.senseipublishing.com and join our newsletter by entering your email address in the pop-up box.

Follow Our Blog: senseipauldavid.ca

Follow/Like/Subscribe: Facebook, Instagram, YouTube: @senseipublishing

Scan the QR Code with your phone or tablet to follow us on social media:

Like / Subscribe / Follow

Introduction

Welcome to the world of the mouse lemur! Little is known about the mouse lemur, but what we do know is that this adorable creature is the smallest primate in the world and is found only in the forests of Madagascar. Here are 30 fun facts about this fascinating animal and its unique habitat.

Mouse lemurs are also known as "dwarf lemurs" because of their small size.

They measure between 4 and 6 inches in length.

Their fur is usually grey or black with white markings.

They are nocturnal, meaning they are most active at night.

They use their long, bushy tails to help them balance when they jump from tree to tree.

Mouse lemurs are omnivores, meaning they eat both plants and animals.

Their diet consists of fruit, insects, spiders, and even small lizards.

Mouse lemurs have excellent vision, thanks to their large eyes.

They can also use their acute hearing to detect predators.

Mouse lemurs are solitary creatures, living alone in the trees.

They communicate using a variety of vocalizations, including chirps, squeaks, and screams.

They use scent marking to communicate and establish territories.

Mouse lemurs have a lifespan of up to 8 years in the wild.

Females build nests in tree cavities for their young.

After 11 weeks in the nest, the young are able to survive on their own.

They are able to go into a state of torpor during the cold winter months, reducing their body temperature and slowing down their metabolism.

Mouse lemurs are prey for many predators, including owls, hawks, and snakes.

They are also threatened by habitat destruction due to deforestation.

Mouse lemurs can move quickly on the ground and in trees to escape danger.

They have a strong sense of smell and can detect food from a distance.

They are adept climbers and can leap up to 5 feet in the air.

Mouse lemurs are native to the forests of Madagascar.

They are found in a variety of habitats, from sea-level to high elevations.

They live in small family groups of up to 12 individuals.

They are important pollinators of many native plants.

They are able to rotate their wrists so that their hands and feet face in different directions.

They have a grooming claw on each hind foot that helps them keep their fur clean.

Mouse lemurs are able to survive in the wild without assistance from humans.

They are important to the health of the ecosystems in which they live.

Mouse lemurs are an important species in Madagascar's biodiversity.

Conclusion

The mouse lemur is a remarkable animal and an important species in Madagascar's biodiversity. With its large eyes, bushy tail, and unique adaptations, this tiny primate is an amazing creature with a fascinating life. We hope you've enjoyed learning about the mouse lemur and its habitat.

Thank you for reading this book!

If you found this book helpful, I would be grateful if you would **post an honest review on Amazon** so this book can reach other supportive readers like you!

All you need to do is digitally flip to the back and leave your review. Or visit amazon.com/author/senseipauldavid click the correct book cover and click on the blue link next to the yellow stars that say, "customer reviews."

As always...

It's a great day to be alive!

Share Our FREE eBooks Now!

kidsonearth.life

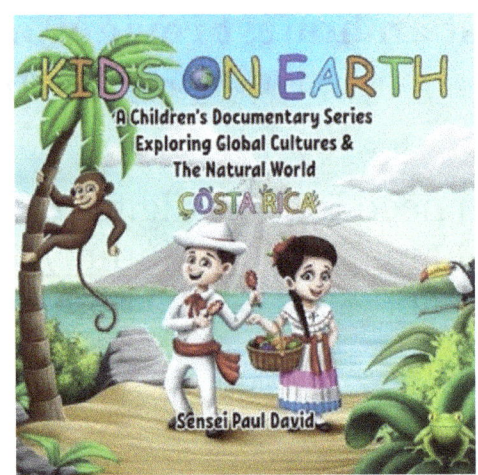

kidsonearth.world

Click Below for Another Book In Each Series

senseipublishing.com/KoE_SERIES

senseipublishing.com/KoE_Wildlife_SERIES

KoE En Español

senseipublishing.com/KoE_SERIES_SPANISH

www.senseipublishing.com

www.senseipublishing.com

@senseipublishing
#senseipublishing

Check out our **recommendations** for other books for adults & kids plus other great resources by visiting
www.senseipublishing.com/resources/

Join Our Publishing Journey!

If you would like to receive FREE BOOKS and special offers, please visit www.senseipublishing.com and join our newsletter by entering your email address in the pop-up box

Follow Our Engaging Blog NOW!
senseipauldavid.ca

Get Our FREE Books Today!

Click & Share the Links Below

FREE Kids Books

lifeofbailey.senseipublishing.com
kidsonearth.senseipublishing.com

FREE Self-Development Book

senseiselfdevelopment.senseipublishing.com

FREE BONUS!!!
Experience Over 25 FREE Engaging Guided Meditations!

Prized Skills & Practices for Adults & Kids. Help Restore Deep Sleep, Lower Stress, Improve Posture, Navigate Uncertainty & More.

Download the Free Insight Timer App and click the link below:
http://insig.ht/sensei_paul

About Sensei Publishing

Sensei Publishing commits itself to helping people of all ages transform into better versions of themselves by providing high-quality and research-based self-development books with an emphasis on mental health and guided meditations. Sensei Publishing offers well-written e-books, audiobooks, paperbacks, and online courses that simplify complicated but practical topics in line with its mission to inspire people toward positive transformation.

It's a great day to be alive!

About the Author

I create simple & transformative eBooks & Guided Meditations for Adults & Children proven to help navigate uncertainty, solve niche problems & bring families closer together.

I'm a former finance project manager, private pilot, jiu-jitsu instructor, musician & former University of Toronto Fitness Trainer. I prefer a science-based approach to focus on these & other areas in my life to stay humble & hungry to evolve. I hope you enjoy my work and I'd love to hear your feedback.

- It's a great day to be alive!
Sensei Paul David

Scan & Follow/Like/Subscribe: Facebook, Instagram, YouTube: @senseipublishing

Scan using your phone/iPad camera for Social Media
Visit us at www.senseipublishing.com and sign up for our newsletter to learn more about our exciting books and to experience our FREE Guided Meditations for Kids & Adults.

www.ingramcontent.com/pod-product-compliance
Lightning Source LLC
Chambersburg PA
CBHW080616110526
44587CB00040BB/3729